Throw,

Disc Golf Humor, , & Tips

Written By aly

Published by EM&EM Publishing
14 South 8th Street
Estherville, Iowa 51334

ISBN: 979-8-89496-393-8
Staten House

Library of Congress Control Number: 2024915244

Printed in the United States of America

First Edition: August 2024

Cover design & illustrations by Emily Mullaly

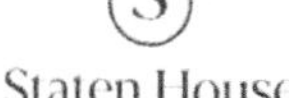

Dedication

This book is fully dedicated to my wife, Emily Mullaly, for this would never have been possible without her putting up with my years of being a smart ass.

I would also like to thank every single member of Team Celestial Discs; you all make me love my job.

I would also like to thank Prodigy Discs for helping motivate me to revitalize my disc golf career as a player, tournament director, and grower of this great sport.

My kids for always being there and caddying for me when I need it.

To my mom…I always knew that when she started having kids in the 70s, she would one day want one of us to become a disc golfer when we grew up.

Do NOT Read This Book If:

- You have a Kyle or Karen attitude…
- You're easily offended or say you aren't, but everyone else says you are…
- You have no sense of humor…

Get ready to embark on a fun, educational journey about disc golf, disc golf, and even more disc golf, which includes some adult and drug humor, pure satire, and a sprinkle of helpful advice, fun facts, world records, and more. Don't take it too seriously—unless you do.

Before we get serious.

If you're a touring pro, would you join Team Celestial Discs for a lifetime supply of tacos?

EAT SLEEP
DISC GOLF
REPEAT

Table of Contents

INTRODUCTION: Why I'm Terrible at Disc Golf, and Why That's Ok!

Disc golf, that excellent hybrid of Frisbee fun and golfing gravitas, has captured the hearts of many. It's easy to get into, won't break the bank, and is a fantastic excuse to avoid actual chores and spend the day outside instead. Despite its charm, I'm here to make a shocking confession: I'm pretty terrible at disc golf sometimes, but guess what? It doesn't even matter.

Here's why:

Outdoor Therapy is Real

Let's face it: one of the big draws of disc golf is that it gets you outside. Think beautiful parks, whispering forests, or vast fields: all perfect for forgetting your troubles—or at least pretending to while you hunt for your off-course disc. Just being outdoors, with the sun on my face and a breeze (hopefully not carrying my disc away), is pure bliss. Whether my disc swoops elegantly towards the basket or detours into Narnia, the scenic beauty doesn't care, nor do I.

Accidental Exercise and Brain Buffing

Disc golf is sneaky. It tricks you into exercising while you're supposedly playing. Trekking from hole to hole, squatting to retrieve wayward discs and the art of the throw are all undercover fitness routines. Plus, it's a mental workout too. It would help if you had strategy, focus, and a lot of patience—especially when your disc seems to have a mind of its own. I may not always hit my target, but my body and brain thank me for the effort.

Class is in Session—Disc Style

Every game is a learning lab. From mastering throws to deciphering disc aerodynamics, it's all about growth. I'm not pro material now, but that's just part of the fun. Each throw is a chance to tweak, adjust, and maybe, just maybe, get a little bit closer to not totally sucking. Improvement is the game within the game, and I'm here for it.

Socially Inept? More Like Socially Invested

Disc golf is the social butterfly of sports. Teaming up with friends, family, or local enthusiasts is common. These gatherings are less about flaunting skills and more about forging friendships. You might be terrible, but so what? Everyone's too busy chucking discs and sharing laughs to worry about it. It's about community, high-fives, and friendly trash talk.

The Art of Embracing Epic Fails

In a world obsessed with perfection, disc golf teaches you to laugh at your blunders and keep swinging—or throwing, in this case. My lackluster disc golf abilities won't land me any trophies, but they teach me to roll with the punches and enjoy the ride. It's a masterclass in humility and the joy of just playing the game.

So, Why Doesn't It Matter?

Being bad at disc golf might sound like a bummer, but it's packed with perks: fresh air, a stealthy workout, continuous learning, social fun, and a healthy dose of humility. So next time my disc decides to explore the wilderness without me, I'll smile and remember—it's not about being the best; it's about enjoying the moment and the quirky, incredible journey of life, one flubbed throw at a time.

101 Pro Disc Golf Tips: A Somewhat Kind of Serious Guide to Elevating Your Game

Pro Tip #1: Grip It and Rip It... Kinda

Have you ever heard someone shout, "Grip it and rip it!" right before they launch a disc into the next county? Well, that's almost right. The key to a perfect throw isn't just gripping it as your life depends on it. Instead, try to hold it like you're cradling a baby bird – firm enough to keep it safe but not so tight that you squish the little guy. Remember, finesse is the name of the game.

Practice your grip with a rubber chicken. It's funny and gets the point across.

Pro Tip #2: Trees are 90% Air

You've probably heard the joke, "Trees are 90% air, and I still hit them." Funny, right? But there's some truth to it. The secret to avoiding trees is visualization. Picture the perfect path and trust in your throw. If you DO hit a tree, just remember it's not a mistake; it's a creative challenge. Or… you take your chance at saying, "I did that on purpose to make my birdie shot look better." I personally will look directly at the tree I'm trying to avoid.

Try whispering sweet nothings to trees before your round. It might not help your game, but it'll definitely improve your mood.

Most Disc Golf Holes Played in 24 Hours: Michael Sale set this record by playing 2,900 holes on September 12-13, 2014, in Spotsylvania, Virginia (Guinness World Record)

Pro Tip #3: The Power of Positive Thinking and Taco's

Keeping your cool during a round is crucial. When your putt bounces off the basket for the third time, take a deep breath and think of your happy place. For many of us, that's a taco place. Imagine the aroma of a freshly baked pizza and let that Zen state guide your next throw.

Actually, reward yourself with tacos after a round. It's a win-win.

Pro Tip #4: The Putt Dance

Putting is serious business, but it doesn't always have to be serious. Develop a pre-putt routine that includes a little dance. Whether it's the personal favorite of hammer time or the Superbowl shuffle, a dance can loosen you up and make those putts more accurate. Plus, it's hilarious for everyone to watch.

Remember, pics, or it doesn't count.

Pro Tip #5: The Magical Disc Quest

Choosing the right disc can feel like searching for a unicorn in a haystack. Pro disc golfers often talk about their "go-to" disc. To find yours, embark on a quest – try as many discs as possible, ask fellow golfers for their magical discs, and don't be afraid to name your discs. Trust me, any disc from Prodigy always flies better.

Listen to your caddy, but if you know, you know.

Pro Tip #6: The 'It Was the Wind' Excuse

Every disc golfer knows the pain of a bad throw. When this happens, remember the golden rule: always blame the wind. Even on a calm day, insist that a sudden gust came out of nowhere. It won't fix your score, but it'll give everyone a good laugh and lighten the mood.

When there's no wind, just say you were expecting wind.

Farthest ace - Caleb Hall of the United States threw the farthest disc golf ace at 611 feet. (Guinness World Record)

Pro Tip #7: The Art of Trash Talk

Good-natured trash talk is an integral part of disc golf. Master the art by keeping it light and funny. Compliment your friend's disc choice by saying it's the best you've seen – since last week. Or, after a lousy shot, remind them that maybe they're just not any good. But then totally cheer them on the next hole as if they're the best to ever play.

Keep a list of pre-approved, non-family-friendly jabs in your bag. You never know when you'll need them.

Pro Tip #8: Rain, Sleet, or Snow – Embrace the Chaos

Real pros don't shy away from a bit of weather. Rain? Extra grip. Snow? Brightly colored discs. Sleet? Wear ski goggles for style points. Embracing the elements not only prepares you for any condition but also earns you major respect points.

Always carry an extra pair of socks. Soggy feet are no joke. I personally bring multiple pairs of shoes also.

Pro Tip #9: The 19th Hole Tradition

The 19th hole isn't just for ball golfers. After your round, gather your buddies and head to the nearest taco joint. Share your heroic shots, laugh about the tree smacks, and plan your next round. The post-game ritual is just as important as the game itself.

Always have fun!

Pro Tip #10: The Never-Ending Journey

The beauty of disc golf is that there's always room for improvement – and laughs. Keep practicing, keep playing, and keep finding the humor in every round. Remember, the journey to becoming a pro is paved with laughter, missed putts, and a whole lot of fun.

Keep disc golf notes if need be or post on social media to keep track—not just for scores but for the hilarious moments you never want to forget.

Pro Tip #11: Find Your Zen Place

Every disc golfer needs a mental refuge – a zen place where they can escape the pressures of the game. This could be a serene spot on your favorite course, a memory of a perfect throw, a dab, or even a quirky mantra that brings a smile to your face. When the game gets tough, close your eyes, take a deep breath, and retreat to your zen place.

If you can't find your zen place, create one by imagining yourself as a disc golf ninja, silently navigating the course with precision and calm. Bonus points if you practice your throws in ninja attire.

Pro Tip #12: Please Stop Complaining

Every disc golfer should focus on the joys of the game instead of the negatives. Constant complaints can dampen everyone's fun. Enjoy what's there; if something bothers you, there's no need to "Karen out" and ruin others' experiences.

Focus on the positives and spread good vibes. Your fellow disc golfers will thank you.

Pro Tip #13: Have Fun

Disc golf is about having fun. You don't need tips to enjoy the game – make bad shots, make good shots, take shots. Who cares? Just have fun!

Embrace the unexpected moments – they often make the best memories.

Pro Tip #14: Disc Golf Therapy

Hanging out with friends, disc golfing, and smoking bowls can be the best therapy. It's a great way to relax and enjoy life.

Laughter and good company are essential ingredients for a perfect round.

Most courses played in 24 hours - Garry Murphy and Joseph Duncan of the United States both played 23-disc golf courses in Illinois on September 23–24, 2018, attempting the record simultaneously and filming the entire 24 hours. (Guinness World Record)

Pro Tip #15: Yell When You're on Fire

When you're playing exceptionally well, it's customary to give out loud yells to assert your dominance on the course.

Develop a signature yell. It adds character to your game.

Pro Tip #16: Kill Them with Kindness

When someone on your card is having difficulty, just "nice" their shots, kill them with kindness (*wink*wink*nudge*nudge) and stay positive.

Stay positive and rise above negativity. It's a win-win.

Why did the disc golfer bring string to the course?

To tie up some loose ends!

Pro Tip #17: Fun is the True Victory

The one who has the most fun is the real winner in disc golf. Enjoy the game and everything it brings.

Prioritize joy over scorecards. It's a game, after all.

Pro Tip #18: Spread the Love

In disc golf, spreading positivity and love to everyone around you is what's important. Everybody loves everybody!

A smile and a kind word go a long way on the course.

Pro Tip #19: Don't Miss

When putting at the basket, focus on not missing. It's a simple tip but a crucial one.

Visualize the disc going in. Positive thinking works wonders.

Pro Tip #20: Avoid the Groove

If you find yourself throwing a Groove, you probably shouldn't. Choose a disc that doesn't suck. Or so they say.

Friends don't let friends throw the Groove.

Pro Tip #21: Hold Your Head High

Hold your head high no matter what happens on the course. Remember, at least you're out there trying. Many people are just sitting at home while you're grinding.

Celebrate your progress, no matter how small. Each throw is a step forward.

What's a disc golfer's favorite type of music?

Heavy metal – for those chain hits!

Pro Tip #22: Get Out and Throw

Get out and throw! The more you play, the better you get. Consistency is vital in disc golf.

Practice regularly to improve your game.

Pro Tip #23: Keep Throwing

When you hit a tree, pick up your disc and throw it again. Persistence pays off in the end.

Every throw is a learning opportunity. Just keep swimming.

Highest altitude round - Disc golfers played a full 18-hole round at a higher altitude, setting up the basket in six different locations with three teeing-off points for each. The original plan was to play at Everest Base Camp, but the golfers moved to a safer nearby village due to dangerous terrain. (Guinness World Record)

Pro Tip #24: Beware the Old Guys

If you see an old guy with a bag full of old discs, get ready to learn a thing or two. Experience often trumps youth.

Watch and learn from seasoned players. Their wisdom is invaluable. Plus, they usually have fantastic stories.

Pro Tip #25: Basket Shenanigans

When your buddy makes a sweet putt, it's customary to quickly take the disc out of the basket and act like it never happened.

Keep the jokes light-hearted and fun for everyone involved.

The highest-rated round of disc golf by the Professional Disc Golf Association is 1132, achieved by Paul McBeth (USA) on 2 March 2013 at the Memorial Championship in Fountain Hills, Arizona, USA. (Guinness World Record)

Pro Tip #26: Don't Listen to Me

Don't take all tips seriously. Find what works best for you and stick with it.

Every disc golfer's style is unique. Trust your instincts.

Pro Tip #27: Use Your Hands

When throwing a disc golf disc, using your hands when you can is best. Sometimes, the most straightforward advice is the best.

Embrace the basics. They form the foundation of your game

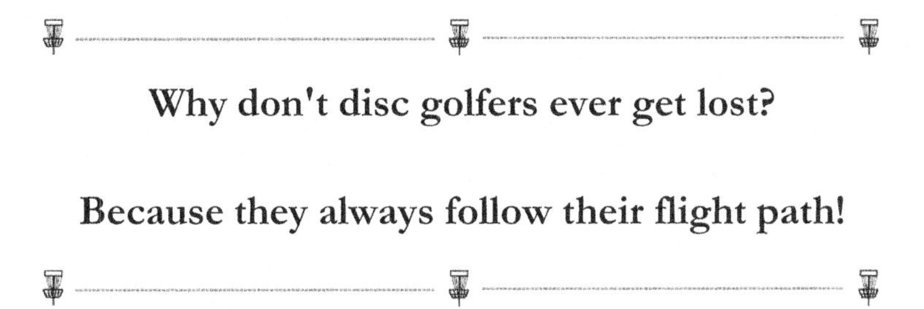

Why don't disc golfers ever get lost?

Because they always follow their flight path!

Pro Tip #28: Leave the Past Behind

Whatever happened on the last hole stays on the last hole. Focus on the present shot.

Concentrate on the current moment. It's the only one you can control.

Pro Tip #29: Kick Dirt

When you make a good putt, it is customary to kick dirt on your buddy's disc as you walk by to clear the basket.

Friendly competition adds excitement to the game.

What did the basket say to the disc?

Catch you later!

Pro Tip #30: Aim for the Basket

You must throw the disc to get it to the basket. Simple but true.

Visualize your shot path clearly before you throw.

Pro Tip #31: It's All Mental

Disc golf is 90% mental and 40% physical. And bud, lots and lots of bud.

Stay relaxed and focused. A calm mind leads to better performance.

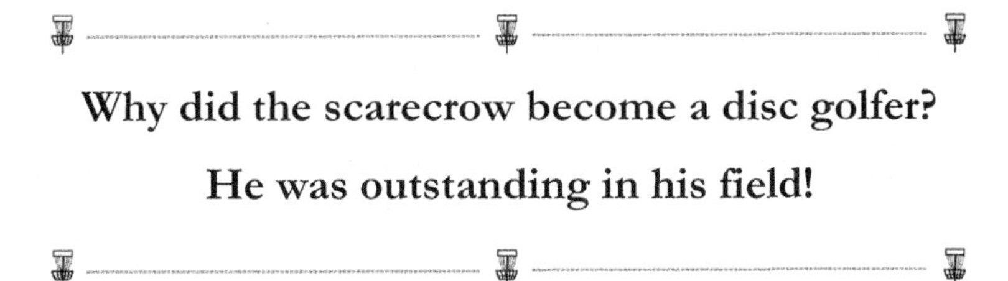

Why did the scarecrow become a disc golfer?

He was outstanding in his field!

Pro Tip #32: Battle Putts

When multiple people have parked shots at a basket, it is customary to suggest battle putts when you walk up to tap in.

Embrace the challenge. It adds fun to the game.

Frolf: Disc golf is sometimes colloquially called "frolf," a combination of frisbee and golf; it is highly recommended not to say frolf.

Pro Tip #33: Be Kind to Your Mailman

Don't be a dick to your mailman, so they take care of your discs when they arrive.

Good relationships with your mail carrier ensure safe disc deliveries.

Pro Tip #34: Lightning Discs

Lightning Discs makes the #1 Driver. Explore different brands and find what suits you best.

Discover what works best for your throwing style.

Pro Tip #35: Skill Isn't Everything

If you're not very good, who cares! It's disc golf. Just have fun. You're out and throwing, and that's what counts.

Enjoy the journey and celebrate the small victories.

Par Ratings: Like ball golf, each hole in disc golf has a par rating, the expected number of throws a player should take to complete the hole.

Pro Tip #36: Call the Crazy Shots

When you throw your disc, and it hits a tree, lands out of bounds, rolls back onto the fairway, stands up with wind, and gains momentum to roll down the fairway, giving you a good drive, it's customary to call that beforehand.

Embrace the unexpected. Sometimes, luck is on your side.

Pro Tip #37: Make the First Throw Count

Make sure your first throw goes in the basket. It's so much easier than putting.

Practice your driving. A strong start sets the tone for your game.

PDGA Membership: As of 2023, the Professional Disc Golf Association had over 150,000 active members (PDGA, 2024).

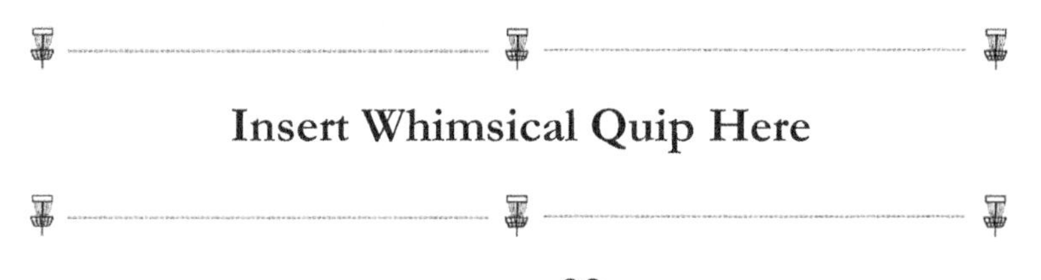

Pro Tip #38: Top Facing Direction

When throwing overhands, your disc will fade in the direction the top of your disc is facing. So, if you're holding the disc with the top facing right, your disc will fade right when it starts to drop.

Master different throwing techniques to diversify your game.

Pro Tip #39: Switch Discs

If you're throwing a disc that isn't doing well for you, throw a different disc. Don't be afraid to experiment.

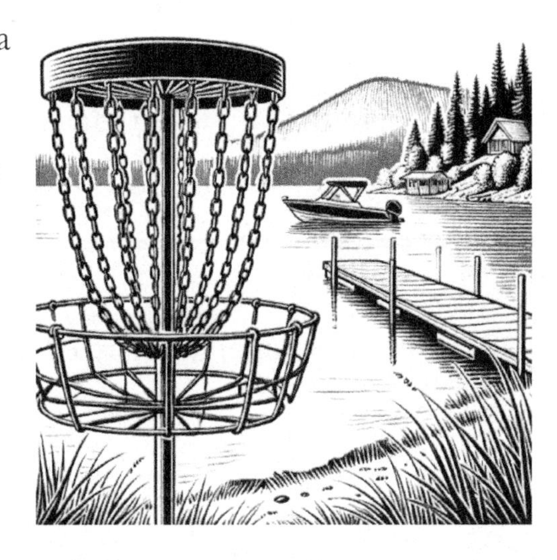

Different discs work for different situations.

First Disc Golf Course: The first official disc golf course was established in 1975 in Oak Grove Park, Pasadena, California.

Pro Tip #40: The Hour Late Guy

If no person in your disc golf group shows up an hour late every time and randomly joins you on a hole, then it's not a true disc golf group.

Embrace the quirks of your group. They make the game memorable.

Pro Tip #41: The Shank Compliment

When your buddy throws a shank straight into the ground, it's customary to look far in the distance and let them know they sure launched that disc.

Keep the mood light with good-natured ribbing.

Discs vs. Frisbees: Disc golf discs are smaller, heavier, and have a sharper edge compared to traditional Frisbees, allowing them to fly farther and with more control.

Pro Tip #42: Respect the Disc Golf Gods

Pleasing the disc golf gods is not a myth but a fact.

Sometimes, little rituals can boost your confidence.

Pro Tip #43: Let the Disc See the Basket

It's always good to show your drivers the basket once in a while, even if it's just the tip, just for a second to show it how it feels.

Visualization can enhance performance. Let your discs dream big.

Tee Pads: Tee pads can be made from various materials, including concrete, rubber mats, and natural grass.

Pro Tip #44: Don't Ask the Internet

Don't ask the internet for recommendations on which disc to throw. Trust your own experience. Personal experimentation is the best way to find your ideal disc.

Only ask the internet if you're looking for bad advice. If you say you're looking to compare putters, one person or five will always name a driver.

The farthest disc golf ace blindfolded is 31.39 m (103 ft), achieved by Joshua Biggers (USA) in Jefferson, North Carolina, USA, on 5 February 2023. (Guinness World Record)

Pro Tip #45: Go with the Unexpected

When in doubt, go back and forth on deciding between two different discs. Then, when you're about to finally throw, grab a third random disc you never considered and nail the shot.

Sometimes, spontaneity leads to the best outcomes.

Pro Tip #46: Start Nicing

When you find yourself losing, just start nicing the other players' shots.

We all know what that really means!

The most wins of the Professional Disc Golf Association World Championships by a female is five, achieved by Elaine King (USA) in 1991–94 and 1997; Juliana Korver (USA) in 1998–2001 and 2003; and Paige Pierce (USA) in 2011, 2013, 2015, 2017 and 2019. (Guinness World Record)

Pro Tip #47: Enjoy the Show

If you throw your disc and some animal other than a dog picks it up and takes off with it, just watch... cause that shit would be so fucking hilarious. Then throw again.

Embrace the unexpected wildlife encounters. They make great stories.

Pro Tip #48: Confirm the Magic

When you make a super sweet putt, it's customary to ask repeatedly if it really went in. "Did that just go in? I didn't see it go in. Did you see it go in?"

Relish the moment. Acknowledge your achievements with a bit of flair.

The highest earnings on the Professional Disc Golf Association Tour are $672,124 (£579,450), achieved by Paul McBeth (USA) as of 12 September 2022 (Guinness World Record).

Pro Tip #49: Plan the Birdie

When you throw a terrible tee shot, make sure to make your next shot for birdie. That way, you can say you did it on purpose to make your birdie shot look better.

Turn mistakes into opportunities for greatness.

Pro Tip #50: Opportunity in Failure

Don't let shanks discourage you. View it as an opportunity to make a sweet-looking up-shot.

Stay positive and creative with your recovery shots.

Pro Tip #51: Distract Your Buddy

When your buddy is teeing off, it is, in fact, acceptable to yell something loud and obnoxious right as they're about to release their disc.

Keep it light-hearted and make sure everyone's in on the joke.

Pro Tip #52: Get Everyone Baked

When you're out throwing with buddies and think you're going to throw badly, just get everyone super baked. That way, they may also throw badly, so it'll all just seem normal.

Equalizing the playing field can make the game more fun for everyone.

Pro Tip #53: Movie Time

When out throwing with your homies, it's customary to reenact Caddyshack while your buddy is trying to putt.

Adding a touch of humor keeps the mood light and enjoyable.

Pro Tip #54: Go for It

Don't be scared. Just go for it! Confidence can be your best tool on the course.

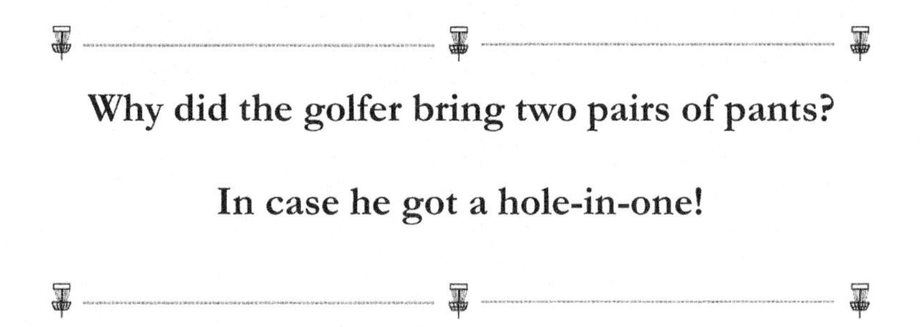

Why did the golfer bring two pairs of pants?

In case he got a hole-in-one!

Pro Tip #55: Listen to Skid Row

If you're not very good and you don't listen to Skid Row, you may have found the reason why.

Find your musical motivation. It can set the perfect mood for your game.

Pro Tip #56: Use Your Feet

When you're walking to the next basket, it's best to use your feet to walk.

Keep moving forward. Every step gets you closer to the goal.

Pro Tip #57: Use Your Dominant Hand

When disc golfing, it's sometimes best to use your dominant hand.

Stick to your strengths while experimenting with new techniques.

Pro Tip #58: Respect the Elements

Pay attention to weather conditions before heading out to play. Wind, rain, and extreme temperatures can significantly impact your game.

Adjust your strategy accordingly. Windy days may require lower, more controlled shots with beefier discs.

Why did the disc golfer quit his job?

Because he couldn't handle the stress of not getting an ace!

Pro Tip #59: Establish a Routine

Develop pre-game rituals to get into the right mindset. This could be stretching, visualizing successful shots, or listening to your favorite pump-up music.

Consistency creates confidence. Stick to your routine before each round.

The most disc golf courses played in one year is 54, achieved by Larry Kirk (USA) in multiple locations in the United States from August to October 2013 (Guinness World Record).

Pro Tip #60: Scout the Course

Before playing a new course, take some time to walk through it and familiarize yourself with the layout. Note any tricky holes or potential hazards.

Pay attention to elevation changes and wind patterns. They can affect your disc's flight path.

Pro Tip #61: Stay Hydrated

Bring plenty of water with you, especially on hot days. Dehydration can lead to fatigue and poor decision-making on the course.

Invest in a quality water bottle or hydration pack to keep you fueled throughout the round.

The most wins of the Professional Disc Golf Association World Championships by a male are 12, achieved by Ken Climo (USA) in 1990–98, 2000, 2002 and 2006. (Guinness World Record)

Pro Tip #62: Fuel Up

Pack some snacks like energy bars or trail mix to keep your energy levels up during long rounds.

Choose snacks that are easy to eat on the go and won't weigh you down.

Pro Tip #63: Cool Down

After a round, take some time to stretch and cool down your muscles. This can help prevent soreness and injury.

Consider using a foam roller or massage ball to target tight spots and promote recovery.

Why do disc golfers make great detectives?

They're always looking for clues (or lost discs)!

Pro Tip #64: Take Care of Your Gear

To keep your discs in optimal condition, regularly clean and inspect them. This includes removing dirt and debris, checking for cracks or warping, and storing them properly.

A good disc golf bag can go a long way.

Pro Tip #65: Know Your Discs

Take the time to learn the flight characteristics of each disc in your bag. This will help you make more informed decisions on the course.

Experiment with different discs during practice rounds to discover which ones work best for your throwing style.

Disc Types: Besides drivers, mid-range, and putters, there are specialized discs like overstable and understable discs to help with different throwing techniques.

Pro Tip #66: Shake Off Bad Shots

Refrain from dwelling on mistakes or missed opportunities.

Instead, focus on the next shot and visualize a successful outcome.

Develop a short pre-shot routine to help clear your mind and stay focused on the task at hand.

The highest player rating for a disc golfer (female) as calculated by the Professional Disc Golf Association is 991, achieved by Paige Pierce (USA) on 13 October 2020 (Guinness World Record). This record was recently broken in 2024 by Kristan Tattar, becoming the first female player to break 1000 rated (PDGA).

Pro Tip #67: Play to Your Strengths

Identify your strengths as a player and use them to your advantage. Tailor your strategy to maximize your chances of success on each hole.

Be honest with yourself about your weaknesses and work on improving them during practice sessions.

Pro Tip #68: Choose Wisely

Consider the risk-reward ratio before attempting a difficult shot. Sometimes, playing it safe is the wisest option.

If you're questioning it, opt for a conservative approach that minimizes the chance of disaster.

DISC GOLF GUINNESS WORLD RECORDS

- The farthest thrown upside-down flying disc by a female is 68.80 m (225 ft 8.7 in), set by Juliana Korver (USA) in Primm, Nevada, USA, on 26 October 2014. The World Flying Disc Federation ratified the record.
- This beat the previous record of 43.83 m (143 ft 9.6 in) set by Jenni Laakso (FIN) in Helsinki, Finland, on 23 July 2006.
- The male record stands at 176.66 m (579 ft 7.1 in), set by Seth Dey (USA) in American Fork, Utah, USA, on 23 September 2021.
- Korver formerly held the record for farthest mini-disc throw (female) and also co-holds the female record for most wins of the Professional Disc Golf Association World Championships at five (won in 1998–2001 and 2003), a title she shares with Elaine King (USA), who won in 1991–94 and 1997, and Paige Pierce (USA), who won in 2011, 2013, 2015, 2017 and 2019.

Pro Tip #69: Get Your Blood Pumping

Start your round with a dynamic warm-up to prepare your body for action. This can include jogging, jumping jacks, and arm circles.

Before the round begins, practice a few throws with each disc in your bag to get a feel for the conditions.

Pro Tip #70: Breathe Deeply

Use controlled breathing to stay calm and focused during pressure situations. Inhale deeply through your nose, hold for a few seconds, and exhale slowly through your mouth.

Practice deep breathing exercises during practice rounds to incorporate them into your routine.

Pro Tip #71: Picture Success

Visualize successful shots in your mind before stepping up to throw. This mental rehearsal can help you feel more confident and prepared.

Imagine the entire flight path of the disc, from release to landing, in vivid detail.

Pro Tip #72: Factor in Wind Conditions

When lining up your shots, pay attention to the direction and intensity of the wind. Adjust your aim and disc selection accordingly.

Watch how the wind affects other players' throws to gauge its impact on your shots.

Chains: The chains on a disc golf basket are designed to catch and stop the disc, making it drop into the basket.

Pro Tip #73: Focus on the Now

Stay in the present moment, avoid dwelling on past mistakes, and avoid worrying about future outcomes. Focus on executing each shot to the best of your ability.

Practice mindfulness techniques to improve your ability to stay present on the course.

Pro Tip #74: Think Ahead

Anticipate potential challenges and plan your approach accordingly. This could involve avoiding hazards, positioning yourself for future shots, or playing for par instead of risking a birdie.

Develop a strategic mindset that considers both short-term and long-term goals.

SEARCHING FOR A

NEW WORLD

Pro Tip #75: Establish a Tempo

Find a rhythm or cadence that feels comfortable and natural for your throwing motion. This can help you maintain consistency and accuracy throughout the round.

Practice timing your throws to a consistent beat or rhythm to develop a smooth, fluid motion.

Pro Tip #76: Learn from Every Round

Pay attention to your performance during each round to identify areas for improvement. Look for patterns or trends that may indicate areas of weakness.

Maybe keep a disc golf journal to track your progress and reflect on your experiences on the course.

Pro Tip #77: Believe in Yourself

Developing confidence in your abilities is crucial for success in disc golf. Focus on your strengths and celebrate your achievements, no matter how small.

Surround yourself with supportive teammates and mentors who believe in your potential.

Pro Tip #78: Welcome Adversity

View challenges and setbacks as opportunities for growth and learning. Embrace the struggle and use it as motivation to push yourself to new heights.

Adopt a growth mindset that thrives on overcoming obstacles and facing adversity head-on.

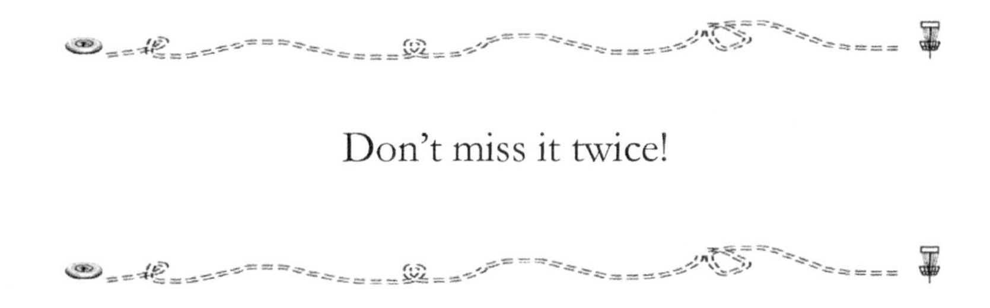

Mini Markers: Players use mini marker discs to mark their lie, or position, after a throw.

Pro Tip #79: Set Clear Goals

Define specific, measurable goals for your disc golf game and develop a plan to achieve them. Whether it's improving your putting accuracy or increasing your driving distance, having clear objectives will keep you focused and motivated.

Break down larger goals into smaller, manageable tasks to make progress more achievable.

Pro Tip #80: Honor Your Competitors

Treat your fellow disc golfers with respect, especially when given respect, for those who don't show respect... just nice their shots. Don't be a dick, and you most likely won't get treated like one.

Pro Tip #81: Adapt to Changing Conditions

Be prepared to adjust your game plan based on evolving circumstances, such as weather changes or unexpected obstacles on the course. Flexibility allows you to remain competitive in any situation.

Stay mentally agile and embrace the challenge of adapting to new conditions.

Pro Tip #82: Stay Calm Under Pressure

Maintain composure and patience, especially during high-stakes moments. Rushed decisions often lead to mistakes, so take your time and trust your abilities.

Practice mindfulness techniques to cultivate a sense of calm and focus during tense situations.

Ace Races: Some tournaments are specifically designed as "ace races," where the goal is to score as many aces as possible.

Pro Tip #83: Enjoy the Process

View each round as an opportunity for growth and self-improvement. Embrace the journey of mastering the sport and savor the experiences along the way.

Celebrate your progress, no matter how small, and find joy in the journey of becoming a better player.

Pro Tip #84: Learn from Every Throw

Don't be afraid to analyze each shot, regardless of the outcome. Reflect on what went well and what could be improved, then apply those insights to future rounds.

Maybe keep a mental or written log of your shots to track your progress and identify patterns in your game.

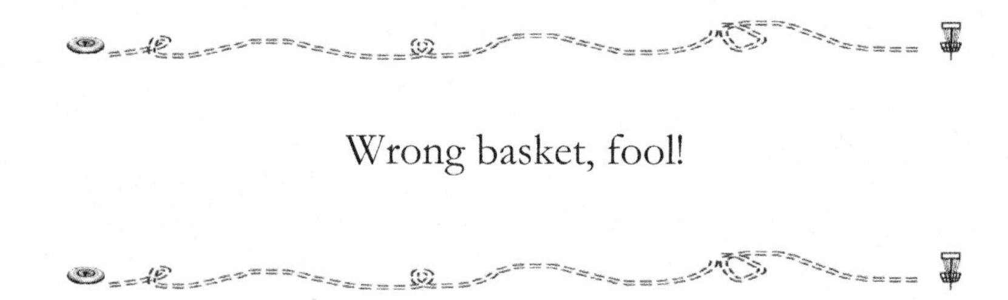

Disc Golf Pro Tour: The Disc Golf Pro Tour (DGPT) is a series of elite professional tournaments.

Pro Tip #85: Master the Basics

Focus on mastering the fundamentals of disc golf, such as proper grip, stance, and release technique. A strong foundation will set you up for success in the long run.

Work with a coach or experienced player to refine your form and iron out any bad habits.

Pro Tip #86: Wear Sunscreen

Protect your skin from harmful UV rays by applying sunscreen before heading out to play. Even on cloudy days, UV exposure can cause sunburn and skin damage.

Choose sunscreen with a high SPF rating and reapply regularly, especially if you're sweating or swimming.

Disc golf is truly the greatest sport no one has heard of.

Plastic Types: Discs are made from various types of plastic, affecting durability, grip, and flight characteristics.

Pro Tip #87: Dress Appropriately

Wear comfortable, weather-appropriate clothing that allows for a full range of motion. Lightweight, moisture-wicking fabrics are ideal for staying cool and dry on the course.

Consider investing in disc golf-specific apparel designed for optimal performance and comfort.

Pro Tip #88: Leave No Trace

Leave the course as you found it, respecting the natural environment and fellow players. Dispose of trash properly, avoid damaging vegetation, and follow any posted rules or regulations.

Pack it in, pack it out!

Consider participating in course cleanup efforts or volunteering with local disc golf organizations to give back to the community.

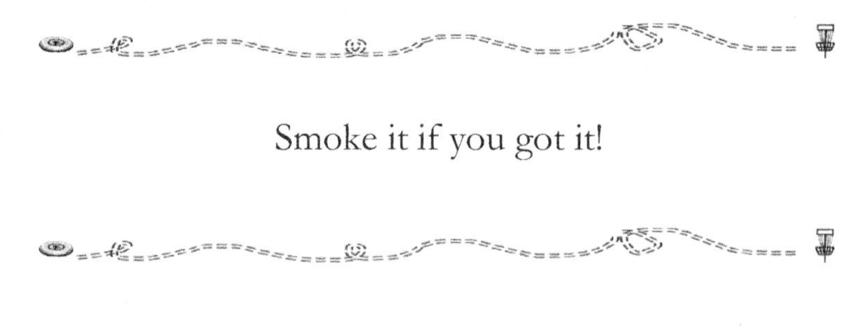

Smoke it if you got it!

Pro Tip #89: Keep Your Discs Organized

Maintain an organized disc golf bag with discs arranged by type, stability, and throwing distance. This makes selecting the right disc for each shot easier and reduces fumbling during rounds.

Sometimes, color-coding your discs can help.

Pro Tip #90: Train for Stamina

Improve your endurance and stamina through regular cardiovascular exercise and strength training. Building physical fitness will help you maintain focus and energy during long rounds.

Incorporate activities like swimming, cycling, or weight lighting into your workout routine to enhance overall fitness and endurance.

Flex Shots: A flex shot is a type of throw where the disc initially flies in one direction before curving back in the opposite direction.

Pro Tip #91: Develop Resilience

Cultivate mental toughness by facing adversity head-on and learning from setbacks. Develop coping strategies for managing stress, anxiety, and self-doubt on the course.

Pro Tip #92: Establish Achievable Objectives

Set specific, measurable goals for your disc golf game that align with your skill and commitment levels. Break larger goals down into smaller milestones to track progress over time.

Celebrate each milestone reached along the way, no matter how small, to stay motivated and focused on continuous improvement.

OB (Out of Bounds): Courses often have designated out-of-bound areas that add penalties if discs land there.

Pro Tip #93: Use Wind to Your Advantage

Learn to read wind conditions and use them strategically to shape your shots. Tailwinds can add distance to your throws, while headwinds require more stability and control.

Experiment with different angles and release points to optimize your throws in varying wind conditions.

Pro Tip #94: Play with Friends

Disc golf is more enjoyable when shared with friends. Invite others to join you on the course for friendly competition, camaraderie, and mutual support.

Organize regular disc golf outings with your friends to stay motivated and connected to the sport.

Pro Tip #95: Limber Up Before Play

Prior to teeing off, incorporate dynamic stretches into your warm-up routine to loosen muscles and increase flexibility. Focus on areas like shoulders, back, and hips for optimal mobility.

Perform dynamic stretches that mimic disc golf movements, such as arm circles, torso twists, and leg swings.

Pro Tip #96: Clear Your Mind Between Throws

Take a moment to reset mentally between throws, letting go of previous shots and focusing on the task at hand. Deep breathing and visualization can help center your thoughts.

Use a consistent pre-shot routine to anchor your focus and maintain mental clarity throughout the round.

Roller Throws: Some players use roller throws, where the disc is thrown to roll along the ground for a distance.

Pro Tip #97: Embrace Course Challenges

View challenging holes or unfamiliar terrain as opportunities for growth and skill development. Embracing challenges can expand your disc golf repertoire and make you a well-rounded player.

Approach new courses with curiosity and a willingness to learn from each experience.

Pro Tip #98: Acknowledge Your Progress

Celebrate your achievements and milestones along your disc golf journey, whether mastering a new technique, achieving a personal best score, or winning a tournament.

Share your successes with fellow disc golfers, friends, and family members who support and encourage your passion for the sport.

Winter Golf: Disc golf can be played year-round, including in winter. Some players use brightly colored discs to find them in the snow or attach a ribbon to the disc.

Pro Tip #99: Learn from Mistakes

View mistakes and missed opportunities as valuable learning experiences rather than failures. Analyze what went wrong, make adjustments, and apply lessons learned to future rounds.

Keep a growth mindset and approach each round with a sense of curiosity and openness to new insights.

Pro Tip #100: Have Fun Along the Way

Remember to enjoy the process of playing disc golf, from practicing in the park to competing in tournaments. Find joy in the sport's camaraderie, competition, and natural beauty.

Take time to appreciate the little moments and connections that make disc golf unique, on and off the course.

Night Golf: Glow-in-the-dark discs and lights on baskets make night disc golf a popular activity.

Pro Tip #101: Share Your Knowledge

Pass on your love and expertise for disc golf by teaching and mentoring others, whether they're beginners or seasoned players. Sharing knowledge fosters community growth and strengthens the sport as a whole.

Offer guidance, encouragement, and support to newcomers as they navigate their own disc golf journeys.

Keep It Fun, Keep It Real

Disc golf is a sport, a hobby, and, for many, a way of life. By injecting humor into your game, you'll not only improve your skills but also enhance your enjoyment. So, next time you step up to the tee, remember these pro tips and let the laughs guide you to disc golf greatness.

Disc on!

The Tale of Fred the Tree Ace

A Fictional Short Story

Fred was known around the local disc golf course as the Tree Whisperer. It wasn't because he could avoid trees but because he couldn't seem to avoid them. Every time he threw his disc, it was as if the trees had some sort of magnetic pull. His friends started calling his discs "squirrel seekers" because they always seemed to end up nestled in the branches.

One sunny Saturday morning, Fred and his buddies set out for their weekly round of disc golf. With his usual good humor, Fred grabbed his favorite driver—bright orange and what he aptly named "The Bark Bruiser." As they approached the first tee, Fred took his stance, eyed the fairway, and, with a mighty heave, sent the disc flying... directly into the nearest tree.

"Timber!" his friend Sam yelled as the disc ricocheted off the trunk and surprisingly landed in the middle of the fairway.

"Classic Fred," Sam laughed.

Undeterred, Fred marched up to his disc and prepared for his second shot. He aimed carefully, trying to avoid the dense cluster of trees ahead. With a smooth release, the disc sailed perfectly—straight into another tree. This time, it bounced off three different branches before miraculously gliding towards the basket, landing just a few feet away.

"Nice tree assist!" shouted his friend Mike.

By the time they reached the ninth hole, Fred was in high spirits. Despite his repeated tree encounters of the first kind, he was having one of his best rounds ever. Then came the infamous Hole 11, notorious for its narrow fairway lined with towering pines.

Fred took a deep breath and threw his disc. True to form, it smacked into a tree with a resounding thud. But instead of dropping to the ground, the disc ricocheted at an impossible angle, soared through the air, and headed straight for the basket. With a satisfying clink, it landed perfectly in the chains.

"ACE!" Fred's friends screamed in disbelief.

Fred stood there, mouth agape, before breaking into a wide grin. "I meant to do that," he said with a wink.

The rest of the round continued in the same fashion, with Fred hitting more trees than seemed possible yet somehow always making incredible shots. By the end of the day, his friends had dubbed him the "Tree Ace," a title he wore with pride.

As they packed up their gear, Fred turned to his friends and said, "You know, I think the trees are just helping me out. They've got my back... or rather, my disc."

And so, the legend of Fred the Tree Whisperer grew, a testament to the idea that sometimes, even when the odds (or trees) are against you, a little bit of luck and a whole lot of laughter can turn any game into a memorable adventure.

If You..., Then You Might be a Disc Golfer.

- If you have more discs loose in your trunk than what you have total in your bag... you might be a disc golfer.

- If you're throwing in a disc golf tournament and care more about having fun than how you finish... you might be a disc golfer.

- If you talk shit to your friends while out throwing but are still rooting them on... you might be a disc golfer.

- If you travel four hours round trip to throw a two-hour round... you might be a disc golfer.

- If you're willing to throw in any event and don't give a shit about your rating... you might be a disc golfer.

- If you celebrate a black ace... you may not actually be a disc golfer.

- If you have a spare room in your house, but it's mainly filled with discs, you might be a disc golfer.

- If you're out throwing with buddies, and one of you misses an easy putt and you yell, "Do better," you might be a disc golfer.

- If you're out in an area and imagine disc golf holes, you could throw... you might be a disc golfer.

- If when you're heading out to run some errands, and you bring your disc golf bag for a "just in case" moment, you might be a disc golfer.

The Classic Disc Golf Excuses Everyone Wants to Hear on The Course!

- The disc must have hit an invisible tree!
- I was testing the wind for everyone else.
- The basket moved after I threw it.
- That was just a warm-up throw.
- I was distracted by a squirrel.
- I was aiming for the tree next to the basket.
- I'm just giving the course a little character.
- The sun was in my eyes… (No sun in sight)
- I was demonstrating what not to do.
- The disc has a mind of its own today.
- I slipped on an imaginary banana peel.
- My arm got a cramp at the last second.
- I was trying out a new throwing technique.
- That was just a practice shot for my real one.
- I was aiming for the scenic route.

Excuses to Give Your Significant Other, So You Can Go Throw!

1. "I really need some exercise, and disc golf is a fun way to stay fit."
2. "I need to show the world my true disc golf potential!"
3. "I've been feeling a bit stressed lately. Playing disc golf helps me relax and clear my mind."
4. "The discs are calling my name, and who am I to ignore them?"
5. "I promised the guys that I'd meet up with them for a round. It's been a while since we've caught up." (yesterday)
6. "I promised the discs I'd take them out today. They get lonely!"
7. "I need some fresh air and sunshine. It's such a nice day, perfect for being outside."
8. "I need to practice my survival skills in case I'm ever stranded in a park with only a disc."
9. "I've been improving my disc golf skills, and I need to practice."
10. "The squirrels at the park have started a league, and they need me to coach them."
11. "There's a small local tournament today, and it's a great way to support our community."

12. "I need to balance out all the time I spend doing chores by mastering the art of disc golf."
13. "Playing disc golf really helps with my mental health. It gives me a chance to unwind."
14. "The disc golf course is the only place where my jokes are considered par for the course."
15. "I need a bit of healthy competition to stay sharp and motivated."
16. "I'm on a quest to find the lost disc of El Dorado."
17. "A new disc golf course just opened up, and I've been dying to check it out."
18. "I heard playing disc golf increases brain power by 10%. I'm doing it for us!"
19. "It's a great way to bond with some friends. We don't get to do this often enough."
20. "If I don't go, the discs will start a rebellion, and I'll lose control of the backyard."

Throw Til the End

A Longer Short Disc Golf Story

The following story is purely fictional.

It was written for entertainment purposes only.

Chapter 1: The Opening Throw

Beep, Beep, Beep!

Kyle sits up in bed, shutting off his alarm at 5:30 am. "Alright, time to do this," he confidently says to the empty room.

Today is no ordinary day; today is Day 1 of the Professional Disc Golf World Championships. The event follows a similar format to a golf major, with participants playing 18 holes daily over multiple days. This year, Pro Worlds is a four-round event with a Finals round on the fifth day, which is only nine holes.

Kyle gears up, making sure his shoes are tight. He grabs his discs and drives to the tournament course for some warm-ups. He has a mixed bag of discs from Prodigy, Dynamic Discs, Westside, and Latitude 64. Each brand complements his well-versed throwing style.

As Kyle arrives at the course, he remains unaware of how the next five days will change his life forever.

Kyle Rudd, a 32-year-old single father, had never imagined himself on this stage. His life revolved around his 5-year-old son, Brian, and his work as a foreman at a local construction company. Disc golf was his escape, a way to cope with the anxiety that often plagued him.

Living in a small two-bedroom house on the edge of open forest land, Kyle found peace in the solitude of the woods. His love for disc golf began over a decade ago, but he had always played it casually, believing he needed to gain the skill to compete professionally. His friends and the local community convinced him otherwise, urging him to sign up for the Professional Disc Golf World Championships.

Kyle kept to himself, practicing his putting. He nailed putts from the edge of the PDGA putting circle with his Prodigy Pa3s and Dynamic Discs Judges. "Damn, I'm feeling it today," he mumbled. He backed up further, barely missing putts from 50 feet. "I sure hope I can keep this up for the tourney."

His dedication to disc golf was unmatched. Every day, regardless of the weather, Kyle practiced. Whether it was putting 100 times daily or throwing at trees in the forest, he honed his skills relentlessly. It wasn't just a hobby; it was his way of managing the stress and anxiety that came with his responsibilities as a single dad and a demanding job.

Kyle's primary motivation was his son, Brian. The little boy was his biggest fan, often accompanying him to the local course. Brian had his own small bag of discs and mimicked his father's throws, creating cherished memories for Kyle. He wanted to show Brian that anything was possible with hard work and dedication.

"At least I had fun," Kyle thought as he headed back to his hotel for the night after spending hours on the course, working on his tee-off game. Winning the tournament would be a dream come true, but his ultimate goal was to make Brian proud.

That night, Kyle decided to hit the hotel restaurant bar to strategize. As he reviewed his game plan, a beautiful woman his attention drew his attention and seemed to keep glancing his way. She smiled when he finally noticed. Timidly, he smiled back, raised his drink, and returned to his thoughts.

Meeting Karen would soon add a new dimension to Kyle's life, offering him companionship and support. But for now, his focus was on the tournament and the promise he made to himself: to give his best and enjoy every moment.

Tee-off time!

Kyle shakes each individual's hand on the card he will be throwing with on Day 1. With disc golf, one throws a round with 3-5 individuals on their card. In this case, Kyle is on a card with four competitors, including himself.

Kyle steps up to the concrete throwing pad to eyeball the hole. It's a 470-foot shot that fades a little left at the end with thick woods on both sides of a cleared fairway. "Backhand time," Kyle whispers as he reaches into his bag and grabs his Dynamic Discs Sheriff distance driver. He does his usual routine: starts at the front of the pad, takes several steps back, gets his feet set, and releases the disc.

"Ugh," you can hear the effort behind the throw as it whips through the air in a nice straight line with a perfect amount of turn as it fades toward the basket.

"That's lookin' good," one competitor says.

"It's going in, it's going in."

Crash! The disc hits the side of the chains and goes out for a near hole-in-one on the first hole of the tournament.

"So close, dude!" one competitor says.

"Well, hopefully, this is a sign of good things to come," Kyle replies to the rest of the group.

The group walks the hole and finishes out, with three of the four competitors getting birdies, including Kyle, whose near hole-in-one landed him just 10 feet away from the basket.

Chapter 2: Finding the Rhythm

Kyle wasn't so lucky on the next hole and only got a par. This was the story of the day for him, with only one other birdie on the round. His only other birdies came on some late holes, leaving him at -4 for the round, with the top round being -10. Roughly about the middle of the field, leaving him roughly around where the last place cash would end up.

He had a rough round with his driving and made all his putts, but he couldn't get off the tee too well with his drives. Putts were dead on, though, including making a few 60-footers to save par on several holes, giving him a glimmer of hope in the days to come if he could clean up his drives. With only one round down, Kyle was feeling confident about his game despite the rough first day.

"At least I had fun," Kyle thinks as he heads back to his hotel for the night after spending hours on the course after his round, working on his tee-off game.

That night, Kyle decided to head to the restaurant bar just outside the hotel so he wouldn't have to drive. "Need to strategize a little bit if I want any chance of cashing out," he once again thinks. Cashing out is just a goal he set for himself for this tourney because he did not want to put his goal too high, just keeping it at a reasonable spot for this is a very prestigious disc golf event with the best disc golfers in the world. He went over the course that he had just played during the day in his head. He needs to tighten up his throws, don't go for it when he doesn't have it, and most importantly… have fun. Having fun is a thing so many players forget to do. It's the key to it all. If you're not having fun, there is no way you will do your best.

While sitting at the bar, reviewing his game plan for the next day, Kyle's attention quickly went towards a beautiful woman who kept glancing his way. He quickly noticed her beauty, and she smiled back at him as she saw that he finally noticed her glancing at him. Being timid, Kyle smiled back, raised his drink at the young woman, and returned to thinking about his game plan.

Beep, beep, beep!

The 5:30 alarm goes off.

Kyle shuts off his alarm, sits up, and realizes how stiff his body is from sleeping wrong. "Damn, this sucks," he expresses while beginning to stretch out his twisted back. Grabbing his gear once again and heading for a quick bite before warm-ups, Kyle starts to go over the game plan for the day in his head in hopes of getting himself focused.

For day 2 of this event, Kyle has to head over to a new course in the same area as the previous day's course. This course is very similar to the previous day, with the course footage being very close and the par being the same at 64.

Putting practice time!

Like the previous day, Kyle was once again nailing his putts from all over, can't miss. "If only I can tune in my drives, I'd have a chance at this," he whispers while practicing. As his back loosens, he heads to the nearest open hole to get some practice drives in before teeing off.

While collecting his discs from his practice drives, Kyle looks around and sees what the other people are doing around the course. In the distance, he swears he can see the same woman he saw last night in the bar.

"Is that her? No way!" he mumbles to himself. "No way! She's a disc golfer?!" Kyle returns to picking up his discs and heading back to his bag.

Thinking no way it could be her and being too far away to chase after her and see, Kyle went on his way in hopes of keeping himself focused for the upcoming day ahead. Feeling warmed up enough, Kyle returned to hole 1, awaiting his tee-off time.

Each group of competitors starts on hole 1. Once the group finishes the hole, a new group steps up to throw, roughly at 15-minute intervals. This gave our competitors an excellent chance to check out some of the throwers on the day and see how they were doing.

During the Professional Disc Golf World Championships, most players are sponsored by some company or another, with a good majority of them being sponsored by the top brands in disc golf. Kyle, however, is not a sponsored player. He just got his PDGA membership just for this event. Don't get me wrong; Kyle is not new to disc golf. He has been playing for 10 years but has not played anything significant.

He only played small events in his hometown, so only locals around him knew of him. It was the locals around him who encouraged Kyle to try this. They always told him how good he was, for he'd never lost a local event. Still, with none of his previous events ever being sanctioned, Kyle never believed himself to be good enough to be a pro. He always thought of himself as just a casual player, one who practices a lot.

Out of all the competitors in the event, Kyle is the last person anyone would ever expect to be there. In fact, he had to wait to sign up and was even on a waitlist, only finding out just days before the event that he was invited to participate.

Back to hole 1, where we await tee off. Staring in awe at all the nice throws, Kyle couldn't believe how good some of these guys threw. "I'm totally out of my league here," he thinks, with pro after pro showing much more talent than him. Watching all the pros from the various disc golf companies that support this wonderful sport, including pros from the manufacturers of discs currently in his bag. "Just focus and have fun," he repeats in a hushed, almost silent whisper.

As tee-off time nears and Kyle's card is up next, Kyle meets his new group of throwers. No one from the day before ended up on his card today, for two of the competitors threw much better than him, and one of the guys he barely beat out just so happens to be on the card following his group.

"Hey Kyle, how's it going, man?" Kyle can hear behind him as he's messing around in his disc golf bag and begins to turn around to see who it is.

"Sup Cam, how are you?" Kyle responds quickly, recognizing the person as one of the competitors from the day before, as someone who he barely pulled ahead of in the scores and ended up on the card following his.

"I'm just hoping I do better than yesterday," Cam laughs. Look out for this guy," Cam starts telling the rest of the card that

Kyle is on. He shows a lot of potential. If he focuses and gets hot, he'll surprise everyone."

Kyle looked surprised as this sponsored pro was giving him such high praise. "Doubt it," Kyle replied, not believing he could really do that.

Time to focus.

Kyle repeats to himself as he grabs his distance driver out of his bag to fill the hole ahead. This hole 1, unlike yesterday, is 450 feet with the basket on the right side of the fairway and back in a little. With this type of hole, Kyle decides to use a sidearm throwing the disc to get the disc to fade right at the end of his drive and hopefully park the hole for an easy birdie shot. In this instance, he likes to use a bit more of what's called an overstable disc to put a little "S" on his throw and ensure the disc still fades to the right for him. So, Kyle carefully decides to throw his Prodigy 500 spectrum plastic d2 pro distance driver for his shot.

Stepping up to throw, last on the card; Kyle concentrates hard on his throw. "I got this," he says as he's about to throw.

Ugh! He puts so much effort into his throw.

"Nice flick, dude," one of the competitors on his card states as he sees the perfectly thrown disc gliding through the air, S-ing out perfectly, and fading right towards the basket like the throw was intended for.

"Nice," another thrower says as the disc lands 20 feet from the basket.

"Sweet," Kyle says, trying not to get too excited over his throw in front of these other pros who do this stuff regularly. Kyle doesn't even play close to as many tournaments as his fellow competitors and definitely never takes courses like the ones he's having the privilege of playing at during this prestigious event. Kyle is definitely a thrower who tends to get slightly more excited when throwing shots like the one he just threw.

While walking down the fairway, Kyle thinks about how he started with a birdie yesterday but couldn't do much afterward. He believes he can do better today by staying focused, trusting his throws a little more, and being more aggressive while still playing smart.

Ching! Kyle makes his reasonably easy birdie putt from only 20 feet away. "Off to a good start again. Let's see if I can get some more birdies today," Kyle thinks while heading to the next hole.

Looking down the fairway at hole 2, Kyle couldn't believe how narrow the fairway was and how thick the woods were on both sides, with a couple of trees in the middle of the fairway as you get further down. "This is going to be tough," he says to the group, and you can tell they are all thinking the same thing. Looking into his bag and contemplating what to throw, Kyle chooses an overhand shot with his Latitude 64 Opto Line plastic XXX, that being his go-to overhand disc.

With the narrow fairway and the basket sitting to the left, he throws it tomahawk style. So, as the disc is thrown, it fades to the left a little bit, and in doing so, our thrower hopes for a little drop and roll out of it, which overhand drives can sometimes do.

Since Kyle threw last on the previous hole and everyone birdied the previous, Kyle was again up last. This may prove helpful because all his fellow competitors on his card hit trees on the hole due to how narrow the fairway is. Allowing him to rethink his shot.

"This hole may be even harder than it originally looked if none of these guys got down there," he thinks while rethinking his decision to go with an overhand throw. Deciding to stick with his original decision and " ignore his caddy," as some disc golfers say, when you rethink your throw. He then eyeballs the hole and makes sure he lines himself up perfectly.

UGGGH!

You can hear all the effort that was put behind Kyle's throw. Overhands take a little bit more oomph when throwing, especially when it's a little bit further away; in this case, it's a 419' hole.

"You got a hold of that one," one of the other guys on the card says while watching Kyle's overhand drive weaves through the trees on the fairway.

"Perfect," Kyle says as he's doing a little Tiger Woods first pump while watching his drive weave through the trees perfectly and get a nice little roll when it lands, which puts him about 35 feet away from the basket. With how he's been putting lately, he'll hopefully walk away with another birdie to go two down after two holes.

After watching the other pros on his card park their upshots for easy birdie putts, Kyle makes it to his disc. Pulling out his main putter, a Dynamic Discs classic blend Judge, Kyle begins to concentrate on his putt to try and walk out of the hole down two strokes.

Ching! He nails his putt from 35 feet out, taking the lead on his card and making him the first to throw for the next hole.

"Starting out better than yesterday, at least," he thinks to himself, taking a little pride in the fact that he just got two birdies in a row during this challenging event.

After watching his competitors make their putts for par, they all head to the next hole. Upon arriving at the hole and checking it out, he saw the girl from the night before. This time, he could tell it was her; this time, he could tell she was carrying a disc golf bag. He thought that was weird, for she most likely wasn't playing at the event because the female pros were throwing the course Kyle threw the day before. "Is she caddying for a male pro" he started thinking. "Her boyfriend, brother, friend… hopefully not boyfriend," he jokingly thinks while focusing on his day ahead.

Stepping up to the tee pad to check out the hole, Kyle notices a water hazard, but the hole is relatively short for his arm, so he pulls out his Dynamic Discs Fuzion plastic Suspect mid-range and gets ready to throw. He releases but released just slightly early. "Uh oh," he exclaims out loud while standing on the tee pad, watching his disc fly straight into the water. "Well, that just erased those two birdies," Kyle says while heading back to his bag to wait for the other throwers to throw.

Since Kyle threw out of bounds into the water, he now has to throw from a drop zone about 150 feet from the basket, with a chance to return to the water. Knowing he has to park this shot and try to walk out of the hole with only a bogey, Kyle decides to go with his Innova Star Gator. Lining up for the shot, Kyle releases a perfectly thrown backhand.

"That's got a chance," one of the other players says while watching Kyle's throw head right for the basket.

Bam! As it slams into the basket for a beautiful save par.

"Heck yeah!" Kyle says out loud as he runs up to get his disc out of the basket so it's not in the way of the other players. "I needed that," he thinks in his head, and he's so happy to be staying two down from par.

From here, Kyle really started taking off for the day. After going four holes in a row with a birdie on each of the four, our thrower sits on hole eight, six down after only seven holes. "Man, I can't believe I'm really doing this," he thinks while walking down the fairway on hole eight and having once again an incredible drive on the par 5 hole. Still having another 400' to go on the hole, Kyle looks it over, for it is a challenging shot. The basket is parked off to the right side of the fairway in between thick groupings of trees that, if hit, will make it very difficult to walk away with a birdie on the hole. Most players tend to lay up straight down the fairway and putt in for the 70-foot birdie shot, so that's what Kyle decides to do here. He is trying to play smart and add to his already impressive round.

"Perfect," the crowd murmurs as Kyle throws his approach shot perfectly, giving him roughly around a 70-foot birdie shot.

Getting up to his disc, Kyle marks his lie with his mini marker. Reaching for his putter pouch, he pulls out his Prodigy 300 spectrum Pa3 for his putt since it is a little bit further. He's used a Pa3 for so long now that it has become his go-to putter in instances like these.

Ching! As he makes an impressive putt for birdie. "Bam," Kyle says aloud while jogging up to the basket to "clear his trash," as some disc golfers like to put it.

Now seven under par after only eight, Kyle can't believe how well he's doing and begins to get a little too excited. He goes on a par streak the next few holes. After a couple of holes, he is lucky to walk away with pars, for he managed to make some excellent putts to save those pars.

Trying to regain his focus and now being on hole 13, Kyle is determined to pull out at least a couple more birdies on the round to finish with a top-notch round. Knowing he can do this after having such a great front nine, Kyle changes things up a little bit by throwing some different discs that he throws less often. This strategy worked out great, for he got a birdie on hole 13 with the help of an incredible drive with his Innova champion metal flake plastic Thunderbird and his Pa3 putter.

Holes 14 and 15 once again birdies, sending him 10 under par for the day and now putting him on the treacherous hole 16, where the hole field has been having issues throughout the day. Hole 16 is a very tough par 3 with a water hazard and lots of out-of-bounds, which has been wreaking havoc on everyone, with only a handful of birdies being made amongst all the other competitors that have played the hole before him.

"I got this," Kyle says, swaggering up to the tee pad full of confidence. Using his Latitude 64 Ballista Pro, Kyle throws a perfectly placed forehand drive just past the water hazard, claiming so many players' discs on the day. Now, trying to avoid all the out-of-bounds on the way to and around the basket, he throws an overhand drive in hopes that it'll just drop right by the basket and not move much by putting a little more loft in his throw. Pulling out his favorite overhand disc, the XXX, Kyle throws a perfect shot landing him 25 feet or so from the basket, which should be an easy putt for him.

"I sure hope I can keep this up," he thinks as he pulls his disc out of the basket after making his easy birdie putt.

"Keep this up, dude. I bet you'll be gaining some strokes on the leaders after today," one of the players on his card told him as they were all heading to hole 17.

With disc golf being such a friendly sport, Kyle has felt he's made friends with the six competitors he's carded with so far during this event. The three from today's card and the three from yesterday. Only playing in his small town, he's never got to see firsthand how awesome everyone is; it's always something he's heard about. Of course, he's friends with everyone back home, but those are the only guys he's ever had the pleasure of disc golfing with. So, he wasn't sure what to expect with an event of this size and caliber.

Getting yet another birdie on hole 17, Kyle heads into hole 18 twelve down on the day. A score that already beat yesterday's top round on the day, so he's hoping it'll be up there today so he can possibly make up some strokes after yesterday's -2.

Hole 18 is yet another very challenging hole on the course, being 368 feet with some really tough out-of-bounds and a small green to land on. Pulling out his fairway driver, a Westside Longbowman, Kyle studies his shot, trying to decide whether to throw a backhand or a flick. With the OB being close to the right side of the basket, Kyle opts to throw a backhand, so it'll fade to the left in hopes of avoiding the OB on the right side of the basket.

Kyle releases his throw, perfect once again, and his disc flies over the right-side OB line to fade right onto the green for another easy putt for birdie.

Clap, clap, clap! Kyle looks behind him to see his fellow competitors on his card and a few spectators clapping, knowing that Kyle will likely finish 13 down on the day. Just applauding the excellent round they just witnessed from a player that barely made it into the tournament.

Raising his hand thanks to the clapping, Kyle heads back to his bag to make his way down the fairway to finish his remarkable round.

After handing in his scorecard for the round, Kyle decides to hang out for a little bit at tournament headquarters. Hoping to learn that he gained some ground on the rest of the competition after yesterday's mediocre round.

As Kyle was hanging out, meeting other pros at the competition, he saw the woman again from the night before. This time, she totally saw him, unlike earlier in the day when he saw her while out throwing his round.

This time, he makes his way to her to say hi because what are the odds he keeps seeing her? Kyle can't help but feel extremely anxious.

"Hi there," he says to her, "I'm Kyle. Are you the one I saw last night at the hotel bar?"

"Yep, that was me," she replied. My name is Karen. It's nice to finally meet you, Kyle." She responded to his question with a big smile.

"Are you caddying for someone?" he asks. "I saw you carrying a bag, but you weren't at the course the females are playing on today."

She then goes on to tell him that she likes caddying for her younger brother at these more significant events to support him and how their whole family came there to support him. After talking for about 30 minutes or so and finding out that Karen just so happens to go to college near where Kyle lives, Karen was forced by her family to part ways so they could all go to dinner. Hoping he gets to see her again, Kyle tells Karen that he hopes they will run into each other again before the event ends.

"Maybe," she replied teasingly as she went to the parking lot to head off with her family.

Upon checking out the scores on the round for that day, Kyle noticed that he had the top round for the tournament at 13 under par. Putting him at 15 under par for the tournament and four strokes down from the leaders

"Great throwing out there," one of the tournament directors told Kyle as he checked out the scores.

"Thank you. I didn't know I had that in me," he told the tournament director. He went on to explain to him that he'd only played in his small hometown for over 10 years, never played other courses outside of where he lives, and never played a larger sanctioned tournament, only just getting his PDGA number the year before.

"That's incredible," the tournament director said, indicating Kyle's impressive feat of having the tournament's best round up to that point.

"Keep it up," the TD continues to tell Kyle. "We may just have a Cinderella sports story on our hands here."

After talking a little longer, Kyle decided to head back to his hotel for the night to relax and focus despite his high anxiety from the day's excitement.

"This is unreal," as he stares at himself in the mirror following a nice long hot shower to relax his body.

After relaxing on the bed for a bit, watching ESPN, Kyle's thoughts drifted towards Karen, whom he officially met earlier in the day. "I sure hope I run into her again; I forgot to get her number," he thinks. Being a bashful guy, Kyle does not usually ask for a woman's number. Still, there was just something about her that gave him the courage and comfort to ask. Determined to ask her when/if he sees her next, Kyle decides to get some sleep, for he's got another big day ahead tomorrow.

Beep, beep, beep!

Kyle's alarm starts going off for the new day. Shooting up out of bed right away and shutting his alarm off, Kyle feels extra good about the day ahead. Since he's only 5 strokes down from the leader, he knows he has an excellent chance of qualifying for the final round tomorrow. There will only be 9 holes on the same course from days 1 and 3.

After sitting in bed for a bit, slowly waking up, and thinking about his day, Kyle starts his usual routine of getting ready and heading to the course to warm up before tee-off. Upon getting to the course, Kyle discovered he was the second to last group teeing off on the day. Apparently, more than a few dropped down in strokes after yesterday's round, and even though the leader gained a stroke on Kyle, he was still sitting in a respectable 7th place at his first-ever major tournament. Which put him on the card just behind the leaders for day 4.

Watching group after group throw ahead of him, Kyle sits there patiently waiting for his card to be up. Confident that he's focused on the day ahead. Still a little bummed about losing his top disc from the day before, Kyle decides to make a quick run to tournament headquarters to see if anyone has turned in his disc. As soon as he arrives at the tent, one of the tournament directors, quickly recognizing Kyle, holds up his disc and shows him that it has been returned.

"Hell yeah! I needed this," Kyle says to the tournament director. "I bagged a back-up for today's round, but it doesn't fly quite like the one I lost." Grabbing his disc and thanking the T.D., Kyle puts the disc in his car and heads back to hole 1 to wait for his card to be up. Since the round had already started and Kyle was not 100% sure of the rules, he decided not to use the disc he just got back to be safe.

Kyle's group was next, with the third to last group now throwing on the tee pad. After the pre-round ritual of meeting your fellow card mates, it was time to throw. Kyle was third to throw on his card, and he was pleased about that, for he got to watch the first two throwers struggle with the high winds that rolled in on the day with the clouds. Watching them gave him a much better idea of what to throw. So, reaching back to his bag to swap out discs, Kyle pulls out a better wind disc for him to use. This paid off, for Kyle had a good drive on the hole, putting him in a decent spot to birdie the hole.

It is Kyle's turn to throw; he pulls out his Judge putter and prepares to attempt his putt in this wind. He was lucky to be in such a good position for a birdie putt, for the other players on his card struggled on the hole. Two threw for par, and another threw a bogey to start their rounds. Kyle hopes to capitalize on having the only birdie shot on the hole.

Kyle putts! Misses! The wind caught his disc in the air and pushed it just enough, causing him to hit the weak side of the chains and bounce out. The chains' weak side is the basket's left side when putting at the basket with normal-type putts from a right-hander.

"Noooo!" Kyle says while picking up his mini, disgusted with his putting on the hole. He's usually an incredible putter from daily practice, but even the wind can mess with a solid putter.

Still walking away with a par on the hole, Kyle and the rest of the group make their way to the next hole. Struggling to figure out this wind, Kyle goes on to par hole 2 and the next three holes, sending him to hole 6, still at even par for the round. Trying to pull it together and remembering that even a par round on the day will most likely send him to the final round tomorrow, Kyle begins to mentally relax a little bit. Now, being slightly more settled, Kyle steps up to throw and releases!

"Got a hold of that," Kyle could hear one of the other players on his card saying as he watched his disc fly perfectly through the air for a beautiful drive that put him in a perfect spot for a birdie.

Coming up on his disc, Kyle pulled out his Westside Discs BT Hard Plastic Harp, which he had bagged before the round began due to the winds. Hoping this disc will be the difference maker in the wind, Kyle nails his putt for his bird on the round.

"Right on! Finally!" Kyle says, jogging up to grab his disc from the basket. "It would be nice to get some more birdies on the round," he thinks as he watches his group finish out the hole.

Now getting himself into a putting groove, Kyle managed to put a string of birdie holes together. Birdieing holes 7 through 11 and bringing him to 6 under par for the round, Kyle comes up to hole 12. A very challenging 1000+ foot par 5 that, on day 2, he was lucky to save par on by making a very far approach shot that went in.

Attempting to give himself a birdie chance on the hole, Kyle starts off great by throwing a bombing drive that landed precisely where he wanted, setting himself up for a good second shot. Coming up to his second shot, Kyle noticed a tree perfectly in the middle of the fairway, leaving him to throw a hyzer shot around the tree to get his throw to where it needed to be.

He releases! Throwing a high hyzer backhand, Kyle did exactly what he needed to do and landed his disc right at the tree line, looking at the basket. About 150 feet left, with a water hazard just short of the basket. Coming up on his disc for his third throw of the hole, Kyle pulls out his Dynamic Discs Fuzion plastic Suspect for a forehand attempt at the hole. Nailing his throw once again, barely clearing the water hazard, Kyle sets himself up for a gimme birdie putt. Only about 10 feet away from the basket, Kyle makes the easy putt to send him to 7 under for the round.

Expecting other groups on the course to have difficulties with the wind as they have, Kyle's card tells him that he's got to be gaining some strokes on the leaders after this. Kyle forces himself to only think about throwing, staying hyper-focused on the moment, ignoring the scores, and taking it one hole at a time.

After the card finishes their putts, they begin to make their way to the next hole, hole 13. Getting a par on the hole and once again on holes 14 and 15, Kyle aims to try and birdie out the rest of the holes in hopes of going 10 under par for the round. He knows it's a far-fetched goal to aim for, but he also thought he would never be where he's at. So why not start to aim a little high.

Stepping up to hole 16, our player checks out the hole and decides to flick his Streamline Trace. Hoping that he can get just the proper fade off his forehand to get around the dogleg right.

Bam! Kyle hits the tree right at the turn in the fairway, trying to snug his drive around to get a good shot and set himself up for an easy bird, still about 175 feet away from the basket after hitting the tree. After everyone did their tee shot, Kyle was next in line to throw, for he was the furthest disc out after hitting the tree. Checking out the shot, Kyle pulls out his Discraft Malta and sets his bag off to the side to get ready to make his throw. Doing his usual routine of setting up his shot, Kyle releases!

"Oh, snap! Get it, get it!" Kyle is heard talking to his disc as it approaches the basket.

Bam! As it nails the basket for a fantastic birdie save.

"Can't believe I just did that."

Clap, clap, clap! The other people on his card start clapping, and the spectators follow their card. Throughout the day, more and more spectators began to make their way toward Kyle's card, for more people kept hearing about the unknown player who was keeping up with the top names in disc golf. It's something you've seen in golf a few times during its long history, but this is the first time it has been seen in disc golf to this extent. The closest is when Nate Doss won the 2005 Disc Golf World Championships.

Getting another birdie on hole 17, Kyle and his card find themselves on the last hole of the day. Not knowing how his score is holding up, Kyle is still going into the hole, hoping to get another birdie to bring him to 10 under par for the day.

Like day 2 of the tournament, Kyle hopes for another lucky birdie on the challenging hole 18. Kyle decides to go with the same driver he previously parked this hole with, pulling out his Westside Longbowman for another forehand shot. Hoping for the same result.

With the wind blowing a lot harder today and blowing from left to right in the direction he's throwing in, Kyle decides to stick with the same disc, ensuring he compensates for the wind. Keeping it a little more left this time, he releases!

"Whoa!"

"What the heck is that" Some guys comment as Kyles's disc starts "dancing" in the wind, trying to fight through it.

"It's going to be close," Kyle says, unsure if his disc will return in bounds. Just barely making it back in, his disc getting a lucky little skip and roll, Kyle releases a big sigh of relief. Knowing he was taking a huge risk by going for such a hard shot, especially in these conditions. He realized he had nothing to lose and everything to gain by taking some risks and hoping they pay off.

After everyone teed off, the group started making their way down the fairway, throwing their discs as they came to them. Only one other person managed to make it to the green in one; two others laid up and played it safe to walk away with pars. Now, Kyle's turn to throw, he pulls out his Westside Discs Harp for the 30-foot putt.

He putts! He nails it! Kyle can't believe it. He just finished the round at 10 under par despite the treacherous wind conditions. Kyle quickly runs up to clear his putt from the basket, showing thanks to all those clapping.

After tallying up scores, Kyle's card mates turn in their cards to the tournament director, and Kyle decides to stick around to see how he compares to the rest of the field. With all but one card turned in on the day, Kyle only has one more group to wait on for scores to see how he's done.

Only a little time passed before the last group started heading into tournament central to hand in their scorecards. Of course, it was the leader's group, so Kyle hoped to make some ground on them. After a short while, the scores were up.

"Heck yeah!" Kyle thinks to himself as he sees he caught up to within two strokes of the leader and is now in third place for the whole tournament with only the final round to go.

"Great job!" One of the tournament directors tells him as Kyle checks out the scores.

Trying to avoid everything and wanting to deal less with social interactions, Kyle returns to his hotel. The anxiety of everything finally hits him as he realizes how big this has become.

Kyle never thought he would have a chance, but it shows that luck and perseverance can go a long way.

While relaxing, Kyle heads to the bar to get a drink to calm his nerves. This is all a little too much for what he's used to. Typically, a homebody, dealing with so much is not something Kyle likes to do, so it's starting to get to him.

Sitting at the bar, watching the baseball game on TV, Kyle glances around the room to check things out. That's when he saw Karen again. She immediately saw him as well and started to make her way over to him.

"May I sit down?" she asks.

"Of course," Kyle replies, trying to stay calm as this dreamy woman asks to sit beside him.

After ordering a drink for Karen, they begin to talk. They talked about everything, and there was instant comfort between the two. She tells him all about her family, job, and life. Kyle also tells Karen about his son, career, and life. Hours went by like minutes.

Kyle learned that Karen is also a disc golfer at the pro level, but she feels she needs to be better to do an event like the Disc Golf Professional World Championships. Upon realizing how late it started to get and knowing he had to get up early for his final round the next day, Kyle says his goodbyes to Karen, ensuring he gets her number. Which she was delighted to give him.

Beep, beep, beep! As the alarm goes off. This is one of the biggest days of Kyle's life. Sitting in third place in the Disc Golf World Championships, not knowing how it will go. Can he deal with the pressure, and will he succeed in winning? Not even Kyle knows what is in store for him on the day.

While doing his regular routine and trying to calm his nerves, Kyle gets ready to go throw.

Chapter 3: Mid-Tournament Reflections

"Only nine more holes to go," Kyle tells himself while looking in the mirror, still extremely anxious but excited at the same time. Once Kyle gets ready, he heads out to get food before his big day.

Arriving at the course, Kyle decides to hang out in his car and eat the breakfast that he grabbed. His anxiety from all the excitement is still high, so he's not quite ready to deal with people yet. After Kyle finishes his breakfast and relaxes, he checks in and gets warmed up for the day ahead.

Today, Kyle is on the leader's card, for he is sitting in only 3rd place for the tournament with only 9 holes left to go. Being day 5, they are back on the course from days one and three. Trying to relax and get focused, Kyle decides to go back to his car and wait for his card to be up. With the parking lot close to the course, Kyle could see everyone tee off. Since only a certain amount of people made the cut for the final day, it was only a short time until Kyle's card was up.

Once he saw his card was up, Kyle made his way over to hole one. He has yet to meet the leaders, so it was quite a treat to meet them since they were three of some of the biggest names in all of disc golf. Kyle, who had only heard stories about these guys, didn't know what to expect. To his surprise, they were just as cool as everyone else Kyle had carded with during this tournament. That's not what he expected from these top pros in disc golf. He expected snobbier people who look down on him, but that doesn't seem to be the case with disc golf; everyone is just super cool in including the top pros. Kyle has definitely learned during his time competing at this event. After meeting everyone on his card and shaking hands with them, it was Kyle's turn to throw.

Unlike yesterday, today is lovely. The sun is shining, birds are chirping, and there is barely a breeze- not too hot, but not too cold- a perfect day for disc golf.

When it was Kyle's turn to throw, he grabbed his disc and stepped up to throw. Releases!

"Oh dang"

"No way"

"Is that going in?" One after another, the people on Kyle's card commenting on his throw.

"Oooooh, come on, baby!" Kyle says excitedly as he watches his disc make an ace run, similar to his drive on the same hole from day 1 of the tournament.

"Go in and stay in this time," Kyle says once again as his disc gets closer.

BAM! Disc nails the basket and stays in.

"Oh my god, oh my god, oh my god," Kyle is cheering, completely in shock about the fantastic shot he just did once again. Kyle cannot believe how many insane shots he's made these past 5 days. Knowing that those great throws are what's given him the chance to be in competition to win this event.

After shaking hands and getting his congrats from the people on his card and the spectators, Kyle grabbed his disc so the others could have a clear basket because they still had to finish the hole. Now officially the most incredible shot of his life, Kyle still can't believe what he has done as he clears his disc from the basket. Still having to wait for the rest of the group to throw, Kyle waits out of the way and watches the others finish out the hole.

Once the group finished the hole, Kyle learned that he was only 1 stroke down from the leader after the leader got a birdie on hole 1.

"I honestly just came here hoping to not get last," Kyle starts telling his group, confessing to these top-notch pros that he's never done a big PDGA-sanctioned event before. Being pro, they can clearly tell Kyle is no stranger to disc golf, even if he is a stranger to larger PDGA events. They can tell right away he must've been playing a long time and plays quite often like they do.

Taking the pad first after throwing the Ace, Kyle gets ready to throw hole 2, only down by 1 stroke. After a great tee shot, Kyle puts himself in another great position to finish the hole strong to keep pace with the leader. With everyone on the card birdieing out the hole, they all find themselves on hole 3. Only seven more holes to go for anyone to have a chance to catch the current leader.

Still having to throw first, Kyle throws yet another incredible drive on hole 3. With the leader up next, he ends up throwing out-of-bounds. Opening up the way for the rest of the card to make a run at the leader spot. With a not-so-great upshot, Kyle finds himself in a challenging position to birdie. Not able to make his tricky birdie putt, Kyle gets a par on the hole. Since going OB, the leader ended up with a bogey on the hole, while the guy in 3rd place took a birdie. Putting the three of them all tied for first in the final round.

With the group matching scores on the following four holes, the leaders still find themselves in a three-way tie for first going into hole 8. Kyle was second on the tee pad at this point, and after watching the first guy throw very well, he knew he needed an excellent throw to match. With no pressure on Kyle, for he was fully content to compete at the top like this, he stepped up to the tee pad and threw a perfect tee shot just like the person before him.

"Sweet," Kyle says in his head after another good drive, keeping him alive and holding on to first place.

The third guy, tied at first place with them, steps up to throw, throwing a great shot along with Kyle and the other leader. Being a par 4 and after another set of upshots, Kyle and his card find themselves all throwing for birdie, with the person in 4th place still being about 90 feet out, looking like a more difficult birdie attempt. Leaving the three tied for first, all around 30-50 feet out. After the 4th place guy missed his birdie putt, it was up to the three tied for first to see if someone could break up the tie. The first of the three was up with a 50-foot putt.

He putts! Misses the putt, hits the weak side of the chains, and bounces out.

Leaving Kyle up next with a 38-foot putt.

Kyle putts! Hits the chains and lands on the edge of the basket. Just wobbling on the edge, not knowing if it was going in or falling out. It was as if time slowed down, and it felt like forever to Kyle as he watched his disc possibly on its way to falling out of the basket.

It falls in! Birdie!

"Oh my god, that felt like slow-mo," Kyle says, sighing in relief. He then jogs up to quickly clear his disc from the basket.

Still tied for first, but with only one other person, Kyle and his card arrive at the last hole of the tournament unless they're still tied after the hole. Then, they would continue on to hole 10 until someone wins a hole. Hole 9 is a challenging par 5 with a water hazard and plenty of out-of-bounds. It starts with having to throw 300 feet to clear the water hazard, and if your disc goes left at all, it'll most likely end up in the water. The first guy steps up and throws a perfect shot over the water hazard and well onto the fairway, leaving Kyle up next. Kyle, opting to throw his MVP Photon, steps up to throw a forehand shot.

He releases! Crushing it, but it starts S-ing out a little more than he wanted. Picking up a wind gust, his disc cuts back to the right, barely making it over the water hazard. If it wasn't such a good, far throw, he would've ended up in the water, where he would've had to take a stroke. After watching the last two people throw, the group makes their way down the fairway to throw their next shots. Kyle had the furthest drive out of the group, so he still had to wait for the other to throw. Now, Kyle's turn to throw, he throws a not-so-great upshot that hits a tree just like the other three people on his card. With the whole card hitting trees while trying to throw through a "jail" of trees, they all found themselves on their 3rd shots around the same area, with an estimated 500 feet left to go on the hole.

Kyle steps up to throw his 3rd shot. Releases! A perfect throw, a hyzering backhand throw, putting him about 70 feet from the basket. The basket sits between a group of trees, with OB about forty feet past the basket. Before too long, it was Kyle's turn once again to throw. With the other leader not too far ahead of him, Kyle knows he's got to go for this shot for birdie. If he misses and the other person makes it, it's over. If Kyle can make this shot, at worst, he ties, and it goes to extra holes.

Contemplating his throw, Kyle decides to go with his Westside Discs Harp. He steps up to his mini and looks over his shot, considering the distance and the little bit of breeze. Kyle releases! Throwing a backhand, aiming slightly to the right of the basket so the disc will have room to fade left and into the basket.

Bam! As Kyle nails his putt for a fantastic birdie putt. Trying to stay calm, Kyle runs up to clear his disc while getting a nice round of applause from all the spectators. Kyle looked around, surprised; apparently, being on the leader's card on the final round of the 5-day event results in having quite a few spectators at this point. Kyle does the calming arm raise thanks to all those clapping, clearing his disc, and returning to his bag to stay out of the way.

"It's not over yet," Kyle goes over in his head, knowing the person he is tied with still has a putt for a birdie.

Pulling out a similar disc to what Kyle just threw, the other leader steps up to his mini to get ready to putt. He putts! It was a similar flight path that Kyle took, aiming a little right so that when the disc fades to the left, it'll fade right into the side of the basket.

Ching! The disc hits the backside of the chains, falls onto the basket's edge, and slowly flops onto the ground.

It's over! Kyle has done it! Kyle is the new Disc Golf Professional World Champion!

Saddened, the other leader walks up to tap in his putt after the rest of the group putts out, getting his par. Kyle walked up to him, shaking his hand, showing his utmost respect to this pro with whom he'd just had this incredible battle until the end. Marking the official end of this prestigious 5-day event that Kyle gave his all.

Loud cheers and whistles from the crowd as they just go wild for what they have witnessed. This person came out of nowhere to win this event. He had never played in a larger PDGA-sanctioned event before and only picked up his PDGA# the year before. He was the last person to get into the tournament, only doing it because he only lived a couple of hours away and was encouraged so heavily by all his friends and family back home. Most importantly, he is doing it for his son, his biggest fan in the world. Doing it for all those who never think they can.

Turning in his card, Kyle continued getting congratulatory handshakes from everyone he saw.

"Congrats, dude."

"Great job!"

"Unlike anything I've ever seen."

One person after another, making sure they get to share in this historic moment.

Hanging around waiting for the awards ceremony, Kyle was relaxing in the camping chair he brought, and that's when he saw Karen through the crowd. Staring right at Kyle, signaling to him to come to her. Of course, without hesitation, Kyle heads straight for Karen, stopping for anyone in the crowd until he reaches her. As he got closer, he started admiring her beauty as she waited patiently for Kyle to approach her.

"Congratulations, champ!" Karen said excitedly before giving him a substantial congratulatory hug.

Kyle decided to hang out with Karen while waiting for the awards ceremony, and the two instantly started talking up a storm. Feeling so comfortable with each other. After some time and making plans to meet up back home and go out on a date, it was awards ceremony time.

First up was the pro women's awards. These women are so great, inspiring little girls worldwide to become professional athletes while doing so much for the sport of disc golf.

Following the pro women's awards were the men's awards. Leaving first place for last made Kyle extra nervous, for he'd have to get up in front of everyone. Walking around and meeting people two or three at a time is one thing, but getting up in front of hundreds of people simultaneously is another.

The prominent tournament director starts to announce, "And your new Professional Disc Golf World Champion, Kyle Rudd!" Kyle walks up to receive his award and winnings, having the biggest smile he may have ever had in his life. A smile so big from the excitement makes his cheeks start to hurt. Kyle doesn't care, though. It's one of the most incredible days of his life, next to his son being born.

Kyle accepted the award with the following speech:

"Wow, this is an incredible honor! I am beyond grateful to stand before you today and receive this trophy. It truly means the world to me. First and foremost, I want to thank my son, my number one fan. Your unwavering support, belief in me, and endless love have been my most significant sources of strength. You inspire me every day to be the best version of myself. This award is as much yours as it is mine. Thank you for being my rock, my cheerleader, and my inspiration. To my friends and family, thank you from the bottom of my heart. Your constant encouragement, understanding, and presence in my life have been invaluable. You've celebrated my successes and lifted me up during the tough times. This journey wouldn't have been possible without each and every one of you. I am deeply grateful to everyone who has believed in me and supported me along the way. This award is a testament to your collective effort, love, and support. Thank you so much for this incredible honor. I am truly blessed. Let me end this by saying I honestly came here hoping to not finish last. I just played my game, stayed consistent, had nothing to lose, and, of course, got some lucky shots."

Kyle knows this was an amazing accomplishment because he got a little help with some lucky shots, and everything worked out so well for him during the five-day tournament.

After accepting his award, Kyle went back to Karen to say goodbye.

"Hope to see you soon," Karen tells him after they say their goodbyes.

"You can count on that," Kyle responds, trying to keep his excitement to a minimum. He feels so lucky to have met someone like Karen at the tournament. Nothing's better than going to play disc golf and walking away after meeting one of the most unique and beautiful women he's ever met.

Chapter 4: The Crucial Plays

Eight months later…

"Daddy, Daddy! I just made my putt from super far away," Kyle's son Brian tells his daddy. He's so excited to have made such a far putt. Kyle and his son are having a wonderful time throwing at trees. Kyle is still thinking about that amazing feat he accomplished eight months ago. His son runs around with him as they go disc golfing in the woods behind Kyle's house.

"Boys, it's time for dinner," Karen yells from the house. Since Kyle's win at Worlds, he and Karen have become quite involved, to the point that she even moved in with him after dating for the last eight months.

Kyle still has his son half the time, is still disc golfing, and still makes sure to get in his putting practice every day while throwing at the trees in the back of his property or at the local disc golf course. Now that he is a sponsored player, Kyle has done more tournaments, getting some wins here and there, but of course, nothing is ever as big as winning worlds.

The next day…

Beep, beep, beep

As the alarm goes off, Karen reaches over to turn it off. "Alright, hun. I'll make us some breakfast, and then let's go get a round in before errands," Karen tells Kyle, trying to wake him up.

"I don't know if I can, babe. I'm not feeling too well," Kyle responds in a sleepy voice.

Leaving him to sleep, Karen makes breakfast for her and Brian before heading out to throw a round at the local disc golf course. After breakfast, Karen and Brian get ready, grab their discs, and head to the car. She told Kyle the plan and that they'd return after their round.

Slam! The front door closes behind Karen and Brian as they head off to throw their round. Kyle then quickly jumps out of bed, preparing to surprise Karen at the course.

Kyle gets to the course but makes sure he parks where Karen and Brian can't see his vehicle so they can't ruin the surprise. While his son and girlfriend disc golf, Kyle secretly follows them without being noticed due to all the growth at the course. He waits for the perfect moment for his surprise, which finally comes on hole 10.

Karen threw an excellent drive that could've been construed as an ace run on a blind hole. Kyle waited at the basket to smack the chains as the disc entered, setting his plan in motion and leading Karen to think she had gotten an ace.

Karen and Brian, excitedly thinking Karen got an ace, quickly made their way down to the hole. As they got closer and rounded the corner of the bushes to finally be able to see the basket, Karen was expecting to see her disc in the basket or at least close to it in case it went in and out. Instead, much to her surprise, she walked up to the basket to find a little box. It was brand new, with a red ribbon holding a little slip of paper that read "Karen." Karen slipped the ribbon off and opened the box to find a beautiful engagement ring inside. Looking away from the ring box, Karen noticed Kyle behind her on one knee.

"Karen, will you please marry me!"

Crying in complete shock and excitement, Karen hesitates to reply. Making Kyle suffer for the surprise.

"Of course, goofball!" she finally replies, quickly hugging him. Brian jumps up and down in total excitement; he's so happy for his dad and Karen.

Walking to the next hole so they can finish the round, Karen turns to Kyle, "Hey, wait! Did I ace that hole or not?"

Roll credits...

Morale of "Throw to the End"

1. **Never Underestimate the Underdog:** Kyle's journey from disc golf weekend warrior to world champion proves that with enough practice, even the guy who's only played against squirrels and trees can surprise everyone—including himself!

2. **Self-Belief is Your Secret Weapon:** Kyle thought pro disc golf was for other people—those who didn't eat cereal for dinner or drive minivans. But guess what? Believing in yourself can make even minivan drivers the heroes of their own sports movies.

3. **It Takes a Village (or a Disc Golf Squad or Team):** Behind every great disc golfer, a crowd of friends, a supportive kiddo, and an incredible lady you meet somewhere. Remember, it's not just about how well you throw but who cheers when you do!

4. **Balance is Key, Just Like in Yoga:** Kyle shows us that juggling disc golf and life responsibilities doesn't mean dropping the ball—or the disc. It's about striking a pose that keeps everything in the air, preferably without pulling a muscle.

5. **Enjoy the Ride, Even if You Throw Your Back Out:** Winning isn't everything; it's also about enjoying the game. If you're

having fun, it doesn't matter if you're hitting chains or chasing discs into the woods. Every throw is a story; some end with less dignity than others. Not everyone wins World Championships and massive kudos to those who do. For the rest of us, just going out to throw wins the game! So just keep throwing!

So, remember, folks, next time you're considering stepping up your game, all you need is a good breakfast, a little belief, and a forest worth of persistence!

About the Author

Eric Mullaly leaves no dad joke untold, seizing every opportunity to share truly groan-worthy puns and nonsensical humor that, somehow, still helps other disc golfers. Despite the humor, his advice is grounded in his decades of experience as both a disc golfer and retailer.

An excellent smack talker, Eric never saw a disc he wouldn't throw at least once and reliably hits at least one tree a month. His favorite go-to discs are from Prodigy Discs, and he is proud to be sponsored by them.

Eric loves growing the sport of disc golf through Celestial Discs, the mom-and-pop store he and his wife, Emily Mullaly, proudly own. This is his first book, and he hopes it will be the beginning of many as he and Emily embark on adding EM & EM Publishing to their ventures.

Connect with Celestial Discs

Facebook: CelestialDiscs

Instagram: @CelestialDiscs

Website: CelestialDiscStore.com

eBay: ebay.com/str/celestialdiscs